LEGO® NINJAGO®
Masters of Spinjitzu

NINJA VS. SERPENTINE

WRITTEN BY
CLAIRE SIPI

SNEAKY SERPENTS

IN SEASON ONE of NINJAGO®: Masters of Spinjitzu a new enemy is unleashed—the venomous Serpentine. A total of 14 amazing LEGO® sets bring the action to life. Turn the page and learn about all the characters—whether they have two legs or none—and meet a very special ninja...

To find out more about this minifigure see p.11.

HOW TO USE THIS BOOK

This book is a guideto the LEGO® NINJAGO® minifigures of Season 1. Learn all about the ninja's amazing skills as they battle the sneaky Serpentine tribes.

CONTENTS

4 Master Wu
5 Cole ZX
6 Jay ZX
7 Kai ZX
8 Zane ZX
9 Samurai X
10 Lloyd Garmadon
11 Green Ninja
12 Kendo Zane
13 Kendo Jay
14 Pythor
15 Lord Garmadon
16 The Great
   Devourer

17 Ultra Dragon
18 Acidicus
19 Fangtom
20 Skales
21 Slithraa
22 Skalidor
23 Bytar
24 NRG Zane
25 NRG Jay
26 NRG Cole
27 NRG Kai
28 Acknowledgments

MASTER WU

CAPTAIN OF DESTINY'S BOUNTY

NINJA FILE

LIKES: Meditating
DISLIKES: Being disturbed
FRIENDS: Reformed brother Garmadon
FOES: Serpentine
SKILLS: Mastery of Elements and Spinjitzu
GEAR: Bo staff

SET NAME: Destiny's Bounty
SET NUMBER: 9446
YEAR: 2012

A very similar Wu minifigure variant with a pearl-gold hat appears in Epic Dragon Battle (set 9450) and Temple of Light (set 70505).

New robes feature snake symbols to protect him from evil—and snakes!

New obi belt is a lighter color than on previous Wu minifigures.

DESTINY JET

After the snakes destroyed the ninja's old HQ, the dojo, the team found a new base in this ancient shipwreck from the desert wastelands. It hides a few surprises—such as the ability to convert it into a flying machine!

CALM AND SELF-DISCIPLINED Master Wu is the perfect teacher. He uses knowledge from years of training to teach the ninja and help them to reach the next three levels—ZX (Zen eXtreme), Kendo, and NRG. In new, lighter, robes he is on the hunt for a new base. Luckily, Cole is the only ninja who gets seasick...

COLE ZX
EARTH ZEN EXTREME

LIKES: The open road
DISLIKES: Punctures
FRIENDS: Zane
FOES: Lasha and all snakes
SKILLS: Driving his Tread Assault vehicle
GEAR: Golden sai blades

SET NAME: Cole's Tread Assault, Lasha's Bite Cycle, Ultra Sonic Raider, Starter Set
SET NUMBER: 9444, 9447, 9449, 9579
YEAR: 2012

DID YOU KNOW?
The Serpentine can be controlled by sacred flute music. Zane and Cole install recordings of this music to play from the Raider, as a secret weapon!

Protective leather-style chest plate

No pauldrons appear on a variant in Car (set 30087).

This three-pronged weapon is the ultimate Serpentine repellent.

ULTRA SONIC TEAMWORK
Cole and Zane take charge of this awesome sonic vehicle, created from recycled parts. Cole drives the tank part, while Zane flies the aircraft that slots on top. With these dual modes, the Raider is the ultimate fighting machine!

THANKS TO HOURS of practice, Cole has achieved the ZX, or Zen, level of his ninja training. To mark his new status, Cole wears silver pauldrons to protect his upper body. As leader of the ninja, it is now Cole's job to help the others develop their own Zen eXtreme skills.

JAY ZX

LIGHTNING ZEN EXTREME

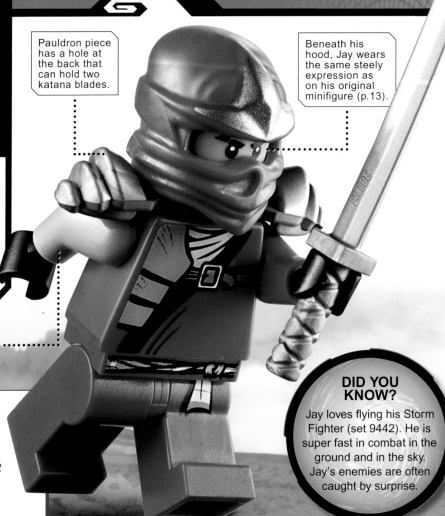

Pauldron piece has a hole at the back that can hold two katana blades.

Beneath his hood, Jay wears the same steely expression as on his original minifigure (p.13).

New robes feature one arm covered in protective silver armor.

ZX ROBES

Jay's new robes help him to be more agile. The light armor is flexible, and without his pauldrons, as in sets 9442 and 30085, he fits snugly into his Storm Fighter, ready to blast through the skies.

DID YOU KNOW?

Jay loves flying his Storm Fighter (set 9442). He is super fast in combat in the ground and in the sky. Jay's enemies are often caught by surprise.

JAY HAS LEARNT many new skills from his teacher, Master Wu. His dedication to learning the ancient martial arts has certainly earned Jay his ZX ninja status. With his new skills, Jay is faster than ever in combat. The enemy won't see Jay's silver blade coming (or the dagger hidden in his robes)!

KAI ZX
FIRE ZEN EXTREME

Removable ZX crown and hood with new gold detail

Protective chest plate worn over red tunic

Throwing stars tucked into belt

SURPRISE WEAPON
In Rattlecopter (set 9443), a Kai ZX variant comes equipped with a unique extra weapon—a jet pack! This useful contraption fits onto a bracket on Kai's back, allowing him to launch a surprise attack over his enemies from above.

Air-resistant adjuster panels

SINCE BATTLING the Skeleton Army, Kai has worked hard to achieve the next level of his ninja training. His ZX minifigure is ready to take on new challenges and enemies. His robes are printed with protective armor, weapons, and two red belts that secure everything in place during battle.

ZANE ZX

ICE ZEN EXTREME

In Hidden Sword (set 30086) a variant of this minifigure appears without golden armor.

NINJA FILE

LIKES: Taboganning
DISLIKES: Emotions
FRIENDS: Dr. Julien
FOES: Pythor
SKILLS: Piloting the flying Ultra Sonic Raider
GEAR: Shurikens of Ice

SET NAME: Venomari Shrine, Fangpyre Truck Ambush, Ultra Sonic Raider, Zane ZX, Samurai Accessory Set
SET NUMBER: 9440, 9445, 9449, 9554, 850632
YEAR: 2012

DID YOU KNOW?

Zane's creator, Dr. Julien, turned Zane's memory switch off, so Zane wouldn't know he was a Nindroid and could live a normal life.

Zane's new robes feature entwined rope belts and a plain white undershirt.

ICE MASTER

The Golden Shurikens of Ice are Zane's preferred weapon. The ZX warrior has perfected his aim with these lethal spinning stars and can even throw them while speeding along on his open-topped snowmobile in set 9445!

Robe edging and armor belt clip printed on legs.

STEALTHY ZANE IS NOW an expert ZX, or Zen eXtreme, ninja. His ZX minifigure features gold pauldrons and gold detailing on his hood. Thanks to the new outfit he can carry two swords on his back, so he can fight more than one Serpent at once! Zane's mastery of the element of ice has also reached an even higher level.

SAMURAI X
SECRET WARRIOR

NINJA FILE

LIKES: Sword practice
DISLIKES: Being told to stay away from fighting, not being taken seriously
FRIENDS: Jay
FOES: Serpentine
SKILLS: Building robots
GEAR: Giant mech sword

SET NAME: Samurai Mech, Samurai X
SET NUMBER: 9448, 9566
YEAR: 2012

Ornamental spiked Samurai crest tops protective helmet.

Nya has already found one of the venomous Fang blades!

Red mask hides Nya's face and true identity.

Protective body armor covers red warrior dress robes and comes with extended shoulder pads.

ROBOT WARS

The Samurai Mech is a massive robot controlled by Samurai X. It comes equipped with a fierce arsenal of weapons—including a cannon shooter, missiles, sharp claws for crushing, and a mighty sword—but will all this be enough to fend off the Serpents?

Samurai helmet conceals Nya in the cockpit.

DID YOU KNOW?

Smart Nya is able to cure a Fangpyre bite and knows that getting just one Fang Blade will stop the Great Devourer!

WHO IS HIDING behind Samurai X's mask? For a while no one knows who this warrior is, but one day the truth is revealed to Jay. Samurai X is Nya, Kai's sister! The ninja are surprised, but soon see that Nya is just as skilled as they are. She might even be able to teach them some things.

LLOYD GARMADON

SON OF LORD GARMADON

Black-hooded cloak is removable.

Golden Constrictai Staff has great power, which makes Lloyd a little wary of it!

NINJA FILE

LIKES: Causing trouble
DISLIKES: Being left out
FRIENDS: Serpentine
FOES: The ninja
SKILLS: Annoying everyone nearby
GEAR: Lightning dagger and golden Constrictai Staff

SET NAME: Lloyd Garmadon, Rattlecopter, Fangpyre Wrecking Ball
SET NUMBER: 9552, 9443, 9457
YEAR: 2012

TWO-FACED
Having the most evil father in all the land is a difficult legacy for Lloyd to live up to. He switches between playing annoying pranks and being scared of his father's powers—as his face reflects!

Green "5" hints at Lloyd's future as the fifth ninja.

LLOYD GARMADON is not as bad as his father, Lord Garmadon. He attends Darkley's Boarding School for Bad Boys and is more interested in candy and practical jokes than plotting to take over Ninjago Island. Young Lloyd accidentally releases the Serpentine tribes and becomes their unlikely leader.

GREEN NINJA
MASTER OF ALL ELEMENTS

DID YOU KNOW?
A magical tea caused young Lloyd to grow older, making him the same age as the other ninja. His legs grew, too!

Pale shirt worn beneath special Green Ninja robes.

Detachable protective shoulder and back armor

NINJA FILE

LIKES: Becoming a hero
DISLIKES: Fighting his father
FRIENDS: The ninja
FOES: Forces of evil!
SKILLS: Wielding the powers of the four elements
GEAR: Golden katana

SET NAME: Epic Dragon Battle, Lloyd ZX
SET NUMBER: 9450, 9547
YEAR: 2012

Silver detailing on robes and belt clasp

KIMONO KEEPSAKE
A variant of the Green Ninja was available exclusively in the original LEGO® NINJAGO® *Character Encyclopedia*. This minifigure had an elaborate, green-and-gold kimono, perhaps hinting at a golden future for Lloyd.

AN ANCIENT PROPHECY foretold that a Green Ninja would rise above all others, to fight the darkness. Surprisingly, the Green Ninja's identity is revealed to be none other than Lloyd Garmadon. The transformative powers of the Golden Weapons turned him into the Green Ninja.

KENDO ZANE

READY FOR ANYTHING

DID YOU KNOW?

Kendo is a Japanese martial art meaning "way of the sword". Fighters wear armor to protect their heads, arms and bodies.

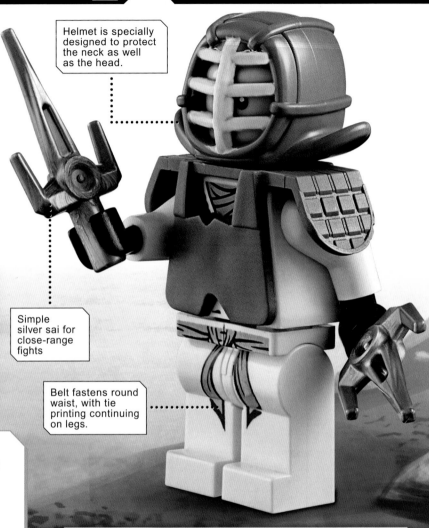

Helmet is specially designed to protect the neck as well as the head.

NINJA FILE

LIKES: Winter sports
DISLIKES: Shipwrecks
FRIENDS: Jay, Master Wu
FOES: Skales, Slithraa
SKILLS: Balancing tricks
GEAR: Silver sai, golden mace, katana

SET NAME: Destiny's Bounty, Kendo Zane
SET NUMBER: 9446, 9563
YEAR: 2012

Simple silver sai for close-range fights

Belt fastens round waist, with tie printing continuing on legs.

MULTITASKING

To master Kendo combined with Spinjitzu while also holding this long golden mace, Zane must have excellent balance.

ZANE IS THE MASTER OF ICE, but in his Kendo outfit he looks more like an ice hockey player! Zane just thinks he looks cool, and is more than ready to take on the Serpentine who are attacking their ninja base—the *Destiny's Bounty*. Zane's armor is lightweight, so he won't sink if he falls overboard!

KENDO JAY
SHIPSHAPE AND SEAWORTHY

DID YOU KNOW?
Kendo fighters use bamboo swords called "shinai" for training. Now an expert, Jay has graduated to a golden blade.

Shoulder pads are grooved and extra-tough.

Golden blade slices through the air as Jay flies in a lightning Spinjitzu tornado!

KENDO HQ
The ninja have plenty of room to practice Kendo on their secret headquarters—the *Destiny's Bounty*. However, when their base comes under Serpentine attack, the ninja have to quickly put their Kendo skills to the test.

ONCE THEY HAVE MASTERED Kendo, the ninja can use any weapons they like. Jay chooses the dark talons and a golden blade as the perfect accessories for his lightning-fast abilities. This new armor doesn't appear to be slowing Jay down at all!

PYTHOR P. CHUMSWORTH

LAST OF THE ANACONDRAI

NINJA FILE

LIKES: Evil schemes
DISLIKES: Getting his hands dirty
FRIENDS: Serpentine minions
FOES: Everyone!
SKILLS: Evil mastermind
GEAR: Fang Blades

SET NAME: Ultra Sonic Raider
SET NUMBER: 9449
YEAR: 2012

Long necks are the Anacondrai's most distinctive feature.

Open-mouthed head with fangs for eating friends and foes alike!

Fangpyre Fang Blade is already in Pythor's possession.

DID YOU KNOW?

While imprisoned, the Anacondrai started eating each other! Pythor ended up a general with no followers, but a full stomach!

NEVER TRUST A SNAKE

When Pythor finally gets his hands on all four Fang Blades, he uses them to release the Great Devourer. His moment of triumph is short-lived—the first thing the Great Devourer does is devour Pythor!

PYTHOR WAS GENERAL of the villainous Anacondrai, the strongest and most feared snake tribe around. After their capture and imprisonment many years ago, he is now the tribe's last surviving member. Pythor wants all four Fang Blades so that he can release the Great Devourer and destroy Ninjago Island.

LORD GARMADON

FOUR-ARMED FOE

NINJA FILE

LIKES: Eating Condensed Evil
DISLIKES: Teamwork
FRIENDS: None
FOES: Great Devourer
SKILLS: Combat skills
GEAR: Golden Weapons

SET NAME: Epic Dragon Battle, Destiny's Bounty
SET NUMBER: 9450, 9446
YEAR: 2012

Removable second torso with two extra arms

Silver torso printing can be seen under the second torso.

DID YOU KNOW?

This version of Lord Garmadon is made up of the same head and body as his 2011 minifigure, with an extra upper body piece.

FACING AN OLD FOE

With his extra arms, Garmadon is the only person able to wield all four Golden Weapons. This surprising ally lends the ninja his many hands in a battle against the Great Devourer—the snake whose bite turned him evil.

HE'S BACK! Having returned from the Underworld, Lord Garmadon still wants to take over Ninjago Island, and also wants revenge on the ninja for thwarting his evil plans. This time he is stronger than ever, with a double torso and four arms! However, his love for his son might just be even stronger.

THE GREAT DEVOURER

KING OF THE SNAKES

LIKES: Eating
DISLIKES: Indigestion
FRIENDS: Serpentine tribes
FOES: Ninja
SKILLS: Eating
GEAR: Super-strong jaws

SET NAME: Epic Dragon Battle
SET NUMBER: 9450
YEAR: 2012

DID YOU KNOW?
Legend has it that the four Fang Blades were created from discarded teeth of the Great Devourer.

LEGO blade pieces make sharp snake fangs.

Printed curved pieces are used to create tough scaly body.

Giant mouth consumes everything it finds.

The Great Devourer's tail is posable.

A BITE TO EAT
Watch out, ninja! The Great Devourer's fang-filled mouth is big enough to hold a minifigure—before crushing and eating it! Let's hope the other ninja come to Jay's rescue in a flash!

THE GREAT DEVOURER was kept safely imprisoned away from Ninjago Island's citizens for many years. Now, Pythor has released the beast from the Lost City of Ouroboros, causing chaos. The giant snake will consume all of Ninjago Island in its terrifying jaws if it is not stopped.

ULTRA DRAGON

FOUR HEADS ARE BETTER THAN ONE

NINJA FILE

LIKES: Independence
DISLIKES: Being controlled for too long
FRIENDS: Green Ninja
FOES: Great Devourer
SKILLS: Firing four missiles at once
GEAR: Four heads, tail

SET NAME: Epic Dragon Battle
SET NUMBER: 9450
YEAR: 2012

DID YOU KNOW?

The Ultra Dragon's four heads come from the Lightning Dragon, the Earth Dragon, the Fire Dragon, and the Ice Dragon.

Handle moves wings up and down

Protective shield is a conical hat piece.

ULTRA RIDER

As the Green Ninja, Lloyd rides the Ultra Dragon to join the battle with the slippery Great Devourer. The ninja use the dragon to distract the snake so that Lord Garmadon can strike the final blow!

THE ULTRA DRAGON is formed from the four Elemental Dragons after they migrate to shed their scales. They return metamorphosed into one mighty, four-headed dragon! This huge creature can flap its wings and flick its tail, and is controlled by the Green Ninja, who rides on its back.

ACIDICUS
VENOMARI GENERAL

Acidicus has two side fangs as well as two front fangs.

NINJA FILE

LIKES: Devious weapons

DISLIKES: Venom shortages

FRIENDS: Other generals

FOES: Skalidor, at times

SKILLS: Inventive mind

GEAR: Venomari Fang Blade

SET NAME: Epic Dragon Battle

SET NUMBER: 9450

YEAR: 2012

All Serpent Generals have a snake tail instead of legs.

ONE OF FOUR

There are four ancient silver Fang Blades, one for each of the four large tribes. Each blade is filled with the venom of its tribe. The Venomari blade has a gruesome green vial of venom at its base.

GENERAL OF THE Venomari Army, Acidicus is very crafty. He has constructed special vials that the Venomari use to carry extra venom in their combat gear, so they never run out of poison in battle. How brilliantly evil! However, no one knows where clever Acidicus keeps his own vials—maybe there are pockets in his tail!

FANGTOM

FANGPYRE GENERAL

Two small heads sprouting from original neck

NINJA FILE

LIKES: Thinking out elaborate strategies
DISLIKES: Disorder
FRIENDS: Skales
FOES: Master Wu
SKILLS: Strong leadership
GEAR: Golden Fangpyre Staff

SET NAME: Fangpyre Truck Ambush
SET NUMBER: 9445
YEAR: 2012

Like all the Serpent Generals, Fangtom has a tail instead of legs.

CAN'T GET THE STAFF

As General of the Fangpyre tribe, Fangtom carries the Golden Fangpyre Staff. A vial of anti-venom tailored to the Fangpyre's unique poison is held in the staff, and its end is twisted like a serpent's tail.

FANGTOM IS THE Fangpyre tribe's general. He accidentally bit himself when he was trying to turn one of his victims into a snake and his poison caused his head to form two smaller heads. Two heads are definitely better than one for Fangtom. He is the brains of the tribe and can cause double the trouble for the ninja!

SKALES

HYPNOBRAI GENERAL

Blue cobra-like hood with hypnotic pattern.

NINJA FILE

LIKES: Seizing control
DISLIKES: Incompetent leaders
FRIENDS: Fangpyre General Fangtom
FOES: Slithraa, ninja
SKILLS: Fang-Kwon-Do
GEAR: Pike, Golden Staff

SET NAME: Cole's Tread Assualt, Destiny's Bounty
SET NUMBER: 9444, 9446
YEAR: 2012

Battle pike can grab and snap other weapons.

DID YOU KNOW?

There is no love lost between the Serpentine tribes, but at one time, the Hypnobrai and Fangpyre tribes were allies.

HYPNOTIC!

Now that he is General of the Hypnobrai Tribe, Skales looks after the Hypnobrai Golden Staff. As the Hypnobrai have powerful, hypnotic eyes, this Staff contains the anti-venom to reverse a hypnotic trance.

THIS COLD AND CALCULATING snake became leader of the Hypnobrai tribe when he beat General Slithraa in a fight. Skales is one of the toughest Serpents around, and is always looking for opportunities to fulfull his ambitions for control and power. He is skilled in Fang-Kwon-Do, an ancient martial art.

SLITHRAA

EX-HYPNOBRAI GENERAL

Without the Golden Staff, Slithraa must content himself with simpler blades.

NINJA FILE

LIKES: A simple life

DISLIKES: Uprisings

FRIENDS: Lloyd Garmadon

FOES: Skales

SKILLS: Giving orders that are never listened to

GEAR: Fang blades

SET NAME: Destiny's Bounty, Slithraa

SET NUMBER: 9446, 9573

YEAR: 2012

Swirling blue and yellow Hypnobrai patterns decorate torso, head, and legs.

DON'T LOOK NOW

Slithraa was the victim of his own hypnosis skills when he attempted to hypnotize Lloyd Garmadon—and his gaze hit a reflective ice surface and backfired on himself! From that moment Slithraa was under the control of juvenile Lloyd, to the displeasure of the tribe.

AFTER HIS HUMILIATING DEFEAT at the hands of his second-in-command, Skales, Slithraa lost his tail and his position as general, and grew legs again. Meanwhile, Skales grew a tail and took Slithraa's place as leader! Demoted to a warrior, Slithraa was forced to swear loyalty to Skales.

SKALIDOR

CONSTRICTAI GENERAL

NINJA FILE

LIKES: Lounging about
DISLIKES: Moving fast
FRIENDS: General Acidicus
FOES: The Ultra Dragon
SKILLS: Sitting on enemies
GEAR: Double-bladed battle ax

SET NAME: Epic Dragon Battle
SET NUMBER: 9450
YEAR: 2012

The general wears a distinctive headpiece with silver spikes.

DID YOU KNOW?

The Constrictai Serpents live underground in caves and tunnels. When they move above ground they are so heavy that they make cracks in the earth.

This weapon is multifunctional—pairing a sharp spear with a double-headed ax.

BATTLE HUNGRY

Alongside General Acidicus of the Venomari tribe, Skalidor leads the epic battle of good versus evil as the ninja, and the Ultra Dragon, take on the Serpentine and the Great Devourer. The snakes want to devour all of Ninjago Island in their hungry jaws!

PLUMP BUT POWERFUL Skalidor is General of the Constrictai tribe. He isn't quite as athletic as the rest of his tribe but he can can crush his enemy with a single blow, or even with the weight of his body. Ninja, don't be fooled by his size—Skalidor's reflexes are fast!

BYTAR

CONSTRICTAI WARRIOR

NINJA FILE

LIKES: Eating, fighting, sleeping
DISLIKES: Baths
FRIENDS: Snike
FOES: Samurai X, aka Nya
SKILLS: Crushing enemies
GEAR: Silver battle mace

SET NAME: Samurai Mech, Bytar
SET NUMBER: 9448, 9556
YEAR: 2012

CATAPULT AMBUSH

Bytar teams up with scout Snike to fight Nya in her Samurai Mech. Using a customized catapult, they can launch missiles—or even themselves—towards Samurai X. This mechanism certainly helps them to reach heights that their legs cannot!

Left eye is scarred from battle.

DID YOU KNOW?
The Constrictai are boa constrictor snakes who attack their enemies from underground hideouts and crush them with their vice-like grips.

Bytar's headpiece is from a different mold to General Skalidor's, and features bright orange spikes.

All the Constrictai have short, stumpy legs.

THIS MUSCLE-BOUND warrior is second-in-command in the Constrictai tribe. Bytar is a bully who likes to work out when he isn't fighting. Unfortunately, he doesn't like to wash, so he does not smell good! Stinky, brutish Bytar eats and beats anything within reach.

NRG ZANE

ICY BLAST

NINJA FILE

LIKES: Icy cold colors
DISLIKES: The color pink
FRIENDS: NRG ninja
FOES: His own memories
SKILLS: Complete mastery of ice
GEAR: Elemental power

SET NAME: NRG Zane
SET NUMBER: 9590
YEAR: 2012

DID YOU KNOW?
Each ninja's "full potential" means something different, and involves finding out who they really are.

Sharp, jagged burst on Zane's chest resembles a powerful blast of ice energy.

Zane is the only NRG ninja to have hands in a different color to his arms.

SECRET PAST

Uncovering his real memories is quite overwhelming for Zane. It takes him some time to adjust to the truth—that he is, in fact, a Nindroid and therefore very different to his ninja friends.

ZANE HAS HAD MANY challenges to deal with, but he is the first of the ninja to realize his full potential. For him, it means learning that he is really a robot—after discovering his memory switch and restoring his memories of Dr. Julien. Having accepted the truth in his heart, Zane is more determined than ever to stop the snakes.

NRG JAY
BOLT FROM THE BLUE

LIKES: Jokes

DISLIKES: Conflicting emotions

FRIENDS: NRG ninja, Nya

FOES: Serpentine

SKILLS: Complete mastery of lightning

GEAR: Elemental power

SET NAME: NRG Jay

SET NUMBER: 9570

YEAR: 2012

Ninja hood is no longer a plain blue, but decorated.

Lightning energy crackles around Jay's eyes.

Jay's NRG outfit features an eye-catching new lightning design emblazoned on his chest.

DID YOU KNOW?
There are still more levels of training to follow NRG status. As well as Spinjitzu, the ninja will go on to learn Airjitzu!

CATALYST
Nya uses her healing skills to heal Jay from his snake-induced injury. By healing him with a kiss, Jay must confront his true feelings—and free both himself and Nya from a snake trap—before unlocking his true potential.

JAY HAS LONG hidden a secret crush on Nya. But it is these feelings that help him to reach his full potential. When he cuts himself on a Fangpyre fossil skeleton and starts to turn into a snake, a kiss from Nya cures him and allows him to achieve his full NRG ninja status.

NRG COLE
SOLID AS A ROCK

NINJA FILE

LIKES: Being in control
DISLIKES: Not progressing
FRIENDS: NRG ninja
FOES: His history with his father
SKILLS: Complete mastery of earth
GEAR: Elemental power

SET NAME: NRG Cole
SET NUMBER: 9572
YEAR: 2012

DID YOU KNOW?
Each of the NRG ninja variants appears in one set only, making their true potential the rarest level of all!

Earth emblem appears in nuclear-bright colors on Cole's new robes.

LIKE FATHER, UNLIKE SON
Cole and his dad share a rocky past. Cole's dad hoped that Cole would grow up to share his profession—dancing. Unwilling to upset him and wanting to become a ninja, Cole ran away. However, after rescuing his dad from Pythor, their relationship is restored and Cole unlocks his NRG status.

Cole's favorite color is actually orange, but his new NRG robes are instead decorated pink.

LEADER COLE is the third ninja to find his full potential. To progress on from Kendo level, Cole must mend his relationship with his father. By way of celebration for achieving this and becoming a NRG ninja, Cole's NRG outfit is much brighter than all of his previous variants—it is black and pink!

NRG KAI
TOO HOT TO HANDLE

Having mastered his element, Kai's eyes glow red with fire energy, not anger or jealousy.

DID YOU KNOW?
Kai is the only NRG ninja to come in a set with another minifigure— Chokun, a member of the Constrictai tribe.

NINJA FILE

LIKES: Being the best
DISLIKES: Helping Lloyd
FRIENDS: NRG ninja
FOES: His own jealousy
SKILLS: Complete mastery of fire
GEAR: Elemental power

SET NAME: Weapon Pack
SET NUMBER: 9591
YEAR: 2012

A red-hot fireball fittingly decorates Kai's NRG robes.

Sparks and flames descend on Kai's legs.

SPIN IT TO WIN IT
Kai tests his full potential in a Spinjitzu battle with the snake Chokun. The Serpentine can also use Spinjitzu skills in battle, but Chokun's powers do not match the well-trained Kai.

TO PROGRESS to the highest level along with his fellow ninja, Kai must learn to control his fiery temper. This is difficult for the hot-headed Master of Fire! When he learns to be himself, without being jealous of Lloyd's Green Ninja powers, Kai is the last, but by no means least, to reach full potential.

Penguin
Random
House

Project Editor Emma Grange
Senior Designers Jo Connor, Mark Penfound
Editors Arushi Vats, Rosie Peet, Matt Jones, Clare Millar
Designers Radhika Banerjee, Dimple Vohra,
Stefan Georgiou
Editorial Assistant Beth Davies
Pre-Production Producer Kavita Varma
Senior Producer Lloyd Robertson
Editorial Managers Paula Regan,
Chitra Subramanyam
Design Managers Guy Harvey, Jo Connor,
Neha Ahuja
Creative Manager Sarah Harland
Publisher Julie Ferris
Art Director Lisa Lanzarini
Publishing Director Simon Beecroft

This edition published in 2017
First American Edition, 2016
Published in the United States by DK Publishing
345 Hudson Street, New York, New York 10014
DK, a Division of Penguin Random House LLC

Contains content previously published in LEGO®
NINJAGO® *Character Encyclopedia Updated and Expanded
Edition* (2016)

003–298874–Jul/17

Page design Copyright © 2017 Dorling Kindersley Limited

ISBN: 978-5-0010-1398-3
Printed in Heshan, China
ACKNOWLEDGEMENTS
DK would like to thank Randi Sørensen, Martin Leighton Lindhart,
Paul Hansford, Madeline Boushie, Simon Lucas, Nicolaas Johan Bernardo
Vás, and Daniel McKenna at the LEGO Group, Gary Ombler for extra
photography, Andy Jones for extra editorial help, Sam Bartlett for
design assistance and Claire Sipi for her writing. For the original edition
of this book, DK would like to thank Shari Last, Julia March,
Ruth Amos, Lauren Rosier, Mark Richards, Jon Hall,
Clive Savage, Ron Stobbart, and Catherine Saunders.
www.LEGO.com

www.dk.com
A WORLD OF IDEAS:
SEE ALL THERE IS TO KNOW